THERE'S A ZOO ON YOU!

By Kathy Darling

The Millbrook Press   Brookfield, Connecticut

Published by The Millbrook Press, Inc.
2 Old New Milford Road
Brookfield, CT 06804
www.millbrookpress.com

Library of Congress Cataloging-in-Publication Data
There's a zoo on you!/by Kathy Darling
p. cm.
Includes index.
Summary: Describes the variety of microorganisms that inhabit the human body, especially the ones that are harmless or helpful, and
how we interact with them in various ways.
ISBN 0-7613-1357-5 (lib.bdg.)
1. Body, Human—Microbiology—Juvenile literature.
2. Medical parasitology—Juvenile literature.
3. Symbiosis—Juvenile literature.
[1. Body, Human. 2. Microbiology. 3. Symbiosis.]
I. Title.
QR171.A1D37 2000
579—dc21   99-047871

The author wishes to acknowledge Martin Weiss, Biology Director, New York Hall of Science, who kindly checked the manuscript for factual accuracy, Louis Diamond, Scientist Emeritus, National Institutes of Health, Harald Linke, Professor of Microbiology, New York University, and Maria Young, University of Texas School of Pediatric Dentistry.

Cover photographs courtesy of Science Source/Photo Researchers (top to bottom: © Francis Leroy, Biocosmos/SPL; © Oliver Meckes; © Dr. Linda Stannard, UCT; © NIBSC; © Dr. Linda Stannard, UCT) Photographs courtesy of Science Source/Photo Researchers: pp. 5 (© Alfred Pasieka), 6 (© Andrew Syred), 8 (© Oliver Meckes/Ottawa), 10 (both © CNRI), 11 (© ArSciMed), 12 (© GABR/Publiphoto), 16 (© Dr. Kari Lounatmaa), 19 (© Francis Leroy, Biocosmos), 20 (© CNRI), 21 (© Dr. Linda Stannard, UCT), 22 (top: © EM Unit, VLA; bottom: © Biophoto Associates), 24 (© Francis Leroy, Biocosmos), 25 (© Oliver Meckes), 26 (© Oliver Meckes), 27 (© K. H. Kjeldsen), 30 (© CNRI), 33 (top: © Omikron; bottom: © CNRI), 34, 37 (© J. Robert Factor), 39 (© Dr. Kari Lounatmaa), 40 (© Dr. L. Caro), 41 (© E. Gray), 42 (© CNRI), 43 (left: © David M. Phillips; right: © Oliver Meckes); © 1994 Richard Wehr/Custom Medical Stock Photo: p. 14; © Dr. Darlyne A. Murawski/NGS Image Collection: p. 17; © Maria Young, University of Texas School of Pediatric Dentistry: p. 35 (top); © Harald Linke, New York University: p. 35 (bottom).

Text copyright © 2000 by Kathy Darling

Printed in Hong Kong
All rights reserved
5 4 3 2 1

YOU ARE NOT ALONE

microorganism
(MY-cro-OR-ga-nizm)
same as microbe—an organism that can be seen only with a microscope.

bacteria
(back-TEER-ee-uh)
one-celled organisms that do not have a membrane surrounding their chromosomes. The singular of bacteria is bacterium.

microbial
(my-CRO-bee-al)   like or having to do with microbes.

microbe (MY-crobe)   a non-scientific word used to describe an organism that cannot be seen with the naked eye.

colony (KA-la-nee)
a group of organisms living close together.

deficiencies
(de-FI-shen-cees)   having less than what is needed.

You are not alone! There's a zoo on you. More than a thousand different species of **microorganisms** live on your body. There are **bacteria**, yeasts, molds, and tiny animals on your skin and hair, inside your nose and mouth, and down in your guts. You have more **microbial** cells on your body than you have human cells! The number of them living on you is so large that it is difficult to imagine. The average ten-year-old, for instance, is home to more **microbes** than there are people on earth.

When you were born you didn't have any of these microbes. Alien life forms began to settle in your sterile body within 6 hours. The first settlers went to your mouth. Before you were 13 hours old, **colonies** of microbes from the air and from things you touched were firmly established in your nose and throat, too. By the end of your first day, invisible organisms had moved into your lower intestine.

Don't be alarmed. It's normal and natural to have resident microbes. These one-celled creatures can't live without us. But here comes a big surprise—we can't live without them, either. Animals and people raised germfree are small and sickly. Without your invisible zoo you would have vitamin **deficiencies**, a weak heart, and you couldn't digest your food. The normal **flora** actually help keep us healthy. Animals without microbes do not have a good immune system. Their bodies have no experience in fighting off **pathogens**. Our zoo of organisms helps us make **antibodies** that we need to kill the dangerous microbes that invade our bodies.

Another surprise is that no matter where you live or what your race or color, you have the same microbes as everybody else in the world. The life that lives on all normal, healthy human beings is the same—regardless of climate, diet, or sanitary conditions.

If, for some reason, you wanted to get rid of your personal zoo, it wouldn't be easy. For one thing, cleanliness doesn't count. In fact, washing only encourages the growth of microbes. A bath, with or without soap, triples the number of skin bacteria for 10 hours. Sure, a good scrub removes microbes that were clinging to the skin. Unfortunately, it also removes sweat and body oils that contain salt and other chemicals designed to kill bacteria. Without competition and

flora (FLOR-a) the microorganisms that naturally live in or on plants and animals.

pathogens (PATH-o-jens) microbes that cause diseases.

antibodies (an-teh-BAH-dees) special proteins made by the immune system to kill germs.

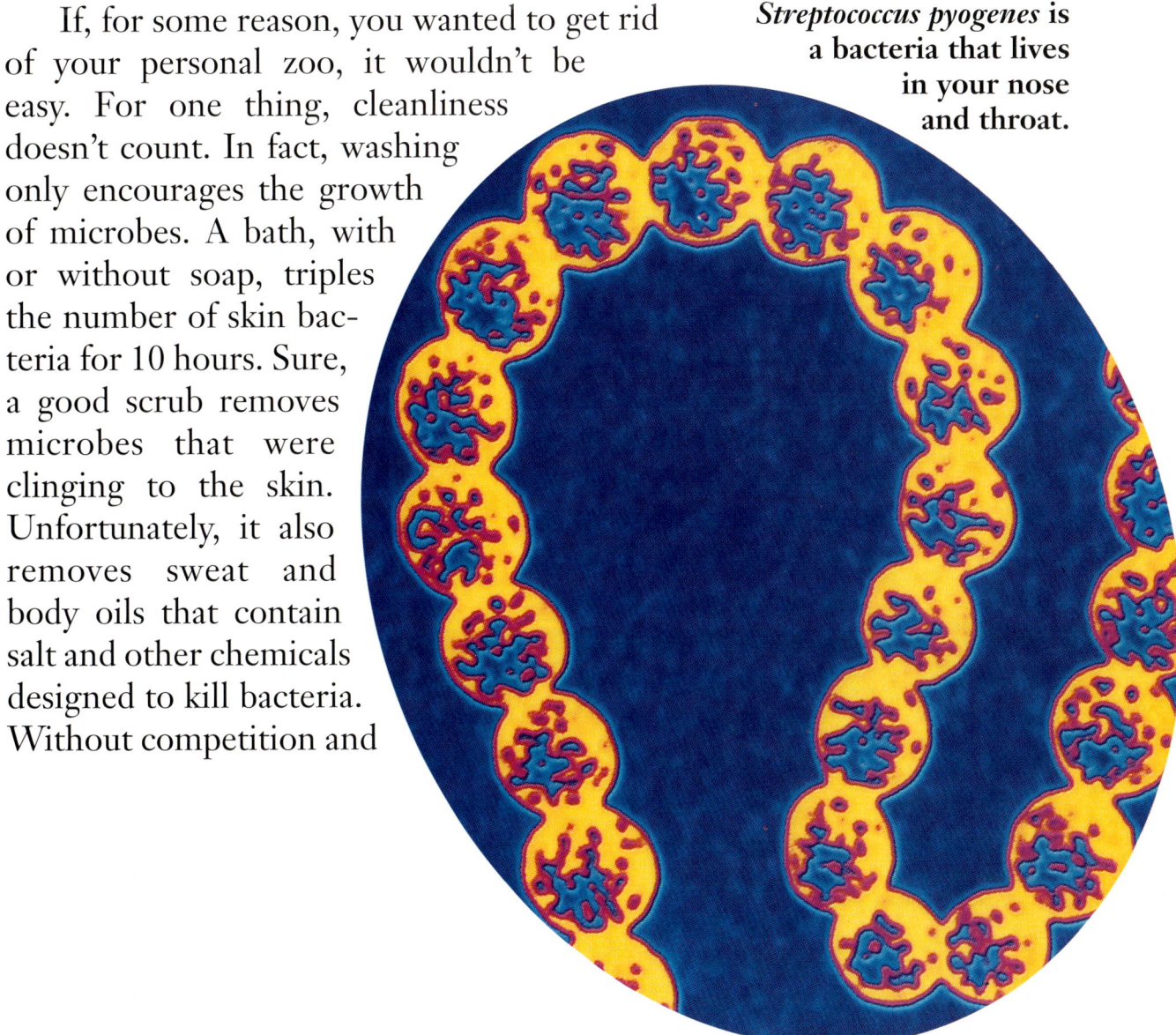

Streptococcus pyogenes **is a bacteria that lives in your nose and throat.**

The rod-shaped *Lactobacillus bulgaricus* may not look like much but it protects you against more dangerous bacteria.

the body's defensive fluids, microbes that were hiding in the nooks and crannies of your skin are free to move in and multiply undisturbed.

An unwashed body does not have any more microbes than a clean one. It may even have less. In a stinky study, kids were asked not to take a bath for four days. (It wasn't hard to get volunteers.) Skin bacteria were counted at the start of the experiment and again when it was finished. Surprisingly, the unwashed kids had half the number of skin bacteria at the end. Seven Arctic explorers participated in an even longer study. Two of them didn't bathe for a hundred days. The others washed at regular intervals. At the end, the bacteria count was the same on all the explorers.

Usually, when you hear about microbes you hear about the **germs**—the ones that make you sick. They get all the publicity, but they make up only about 4 percent of the microbial population. Most microorganisms are harmless. A few are actually helpful. Those harmless or helpful microbes are called **commensals**, and this book is about them.

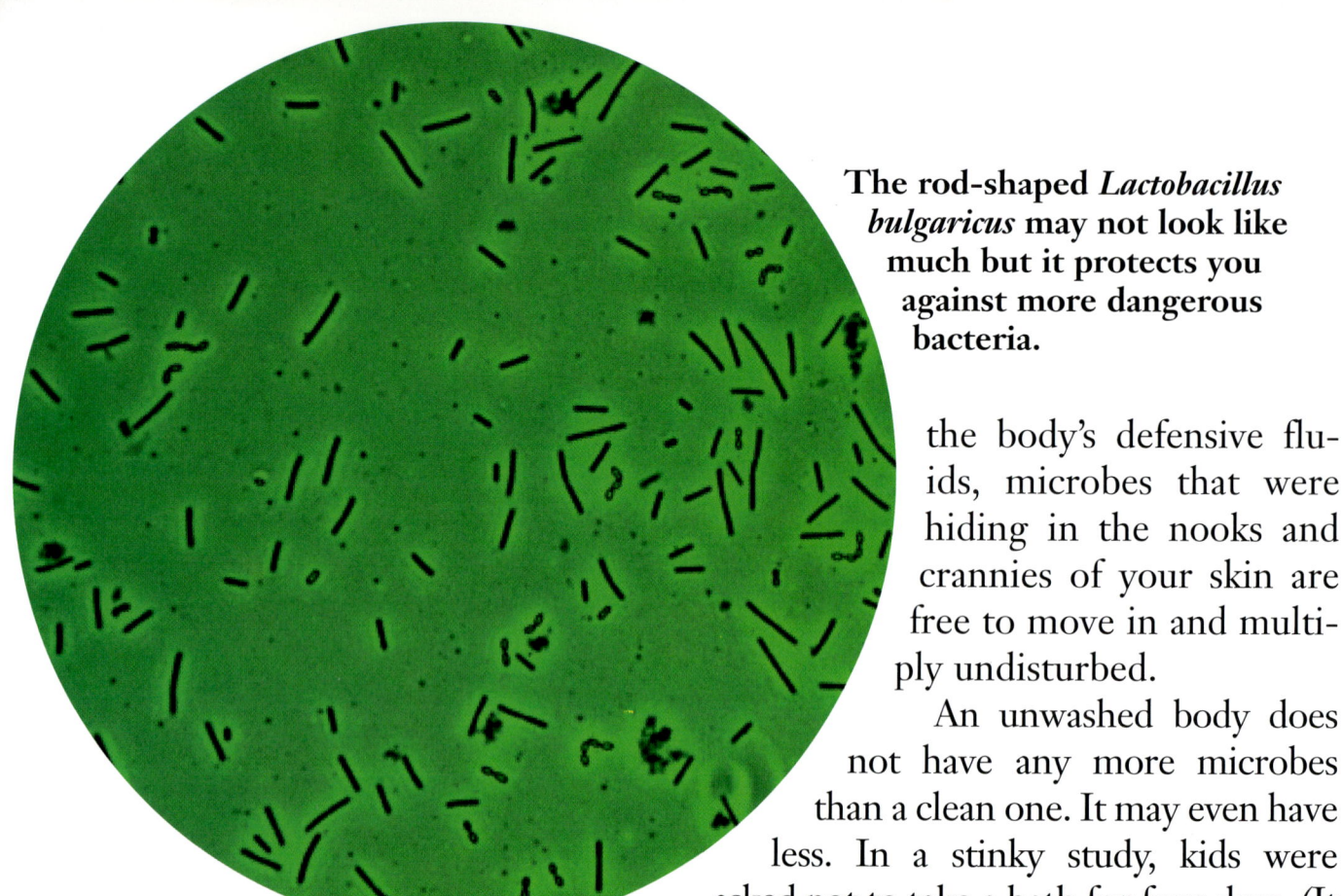

germ (jurm) refers to all microorganisms, although usually the bacteria and viruses that cause disease.

commensals (ko-MEN-sals) two organisms of different species that live together and share food. One species benefits, and the other is not harmed.

CLASSIFYING YOUR MICRO ZOO

There are five kingdoms of living things: **Monera, Protista, Fungi, Plants, and Animals. Viruses** have some of the characteristics of living things and are often included as a sixth group.

Five of these kingdoms have members in your personal zoo.

Monera came first, billions of years ago. They are always one-celled and don't have a nucleus. Most members of the zoo on you are monera because bacteria belong to this kingdom.

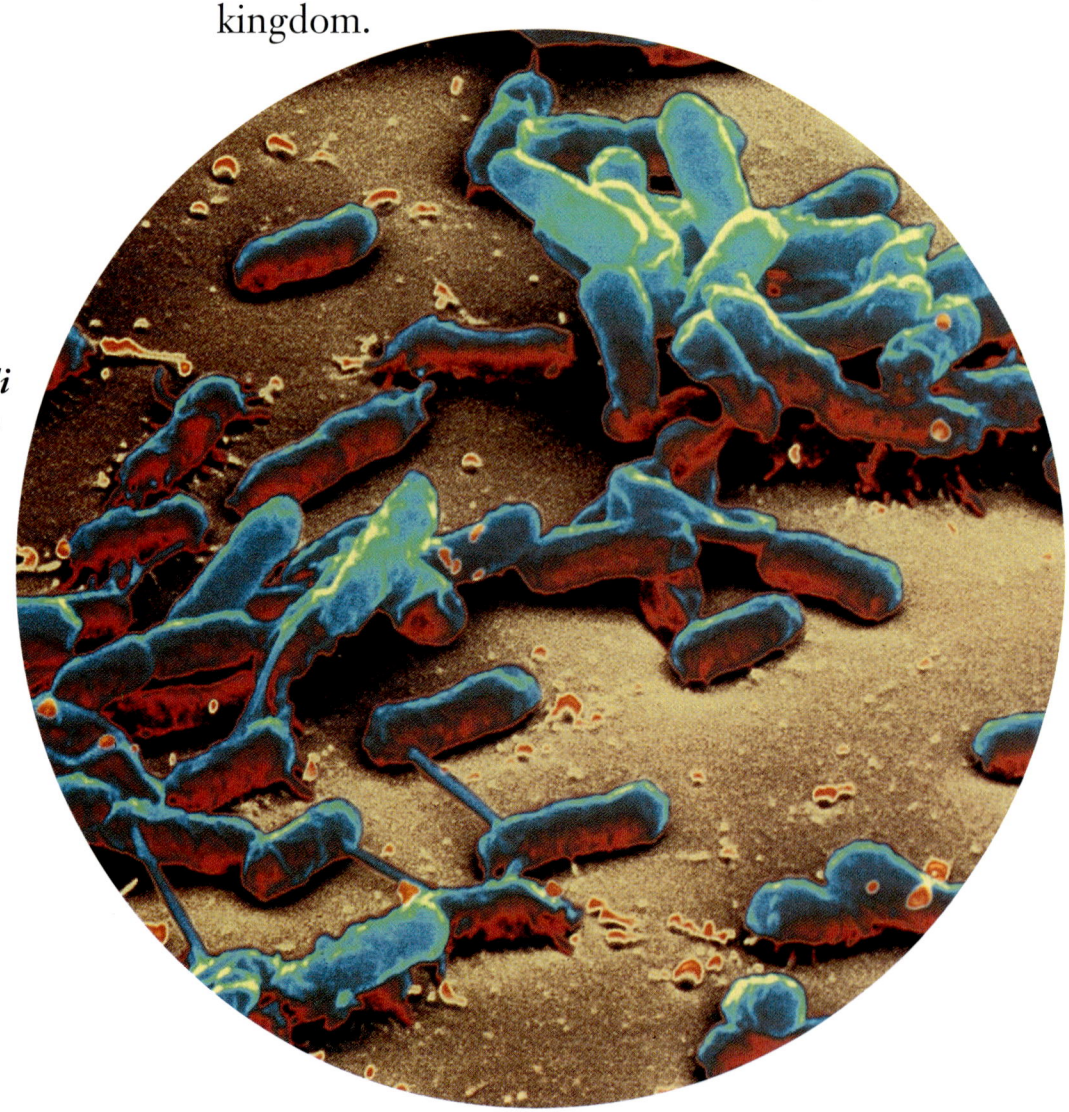

Escherichia coli **is part of the single-celled** *Monera* **kingdom.**

Protista appeared after the bacteria, but still billions of years ago. Their cells contain a nucleus. Single-celled protista are called protists. These creatures are capable of a wide range of activities such as "house" construction, food processing, and "walking." Your amoeba commensals are protists.

Fungi are **organisms** that may be one-celled or multicelled. They can be large or microscopic. Mushrooms and toadstools are members of the fungi kingdom. So are the yeasts and molds that live in your zoo. Fungi cannot make their own food. They absorb nutrients from water or from the tissue of creatures like you.

Plants are not members of the microscopic zoo on you. Plants would find no benefit from colonizing humans. Most of our zoo microbes want to use us as food. Plants, which are always multicelled, don't eat other living things. As long as there is sunlight, they can make their own food.

Animals can be divided into two subgroups. Metazoa are large, multicelled animals, such as humans. Protozoa are one-celled animals like the mites in your eyelashes. In the simplest definition, animals are organisms that move.

Viruses are the smallest known reproducing beings. Scientists are not sure whether they should be classified as living creatures, because viruses cannot reproduce

organism
(OR-ga-nizm)
an individual living thing.

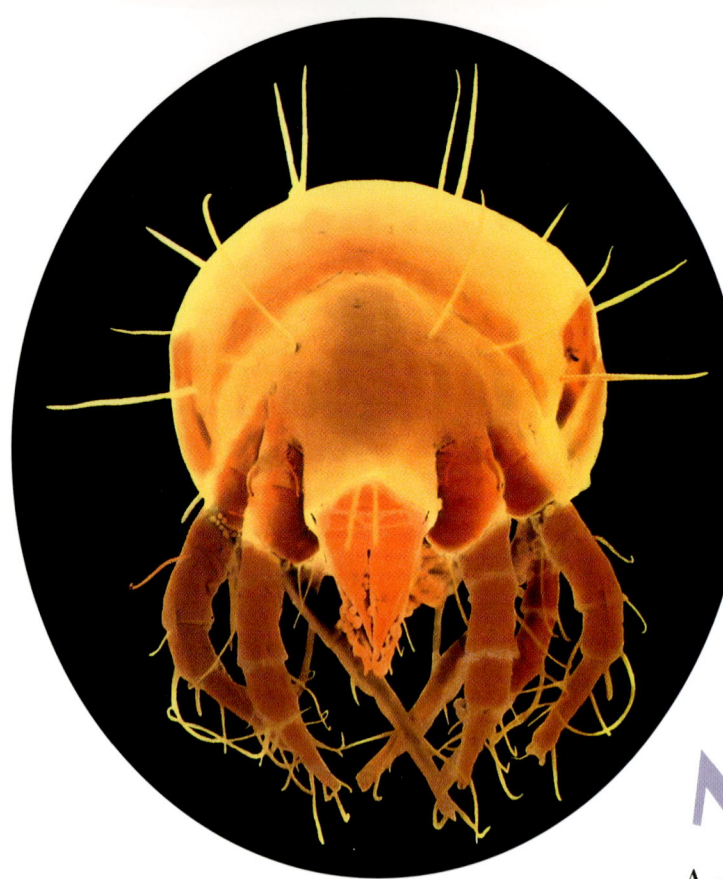

outside of a living cell. Your normal flora includes several viruses, including the one that makes warts.

SIZE

The zoo on you is very small. So small, in fact, that special measurements had to be invented to describe it.

MICRONS

A micron is a unit of linear measure. The symbol for micron is µ. One µ is equal to 1/1000 of a millimeter. This is a square millimeter:

.

You can't see anything as small as a micron without a microscope. The smallest thing visible to the human eye is about 200µ.

Mites and amoebas are giants in the world of microbes. Their average size is 100µ.

Yeasts often form large colonies that you can see with the naked eye. The average size of a single yeast organism is 5 to 10µ.

Most bacteria which are individually 1 to 5 µ form colonies. These groups, sometimes brightly colored, are visible.

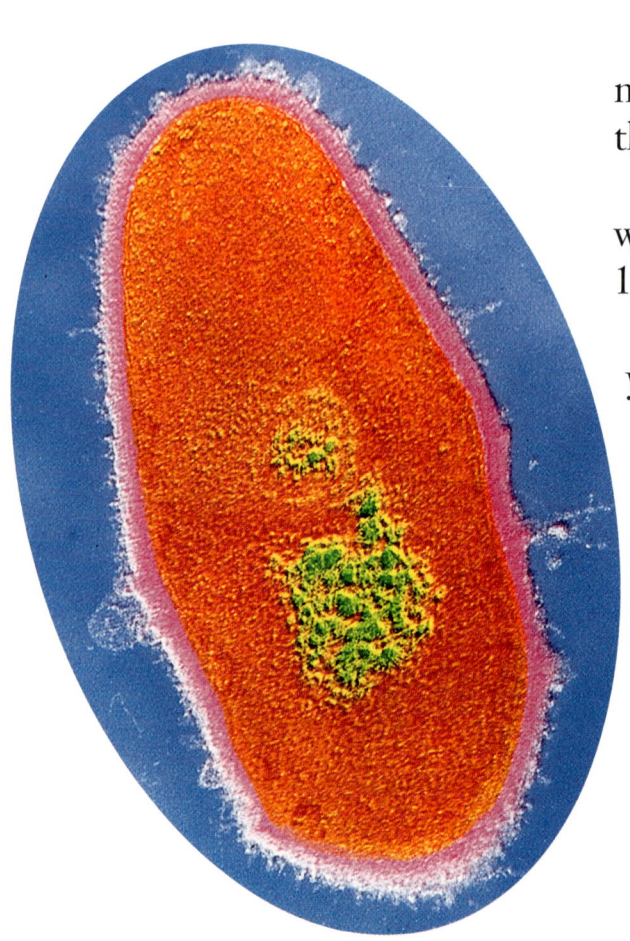

This mite is shown 343 times it's size.

This bacteria is shown 120,000 times it's size.

Viruses range greatly in size. The average size is 1/50 of a µ, but some of them are even larger than the smallest bacteria.

Things this tiny are hard to visualize. It might help if you think of the size relationship between microbes this way: If a mite were the size of an elephant, then a bacterium would be the size of a flea and a virus would be the size of a speck of dust.

SQUARE CENTIMETER

Scientists who need to count microbes use the square centimeter as a measure. Here is a square centimeter: ■

Sometimes it is not easy to calculate the population of microbes living in one of these squares. Trillions of some species could fit inside it.

ABOUT THE PICTURES IN THIS BOOK

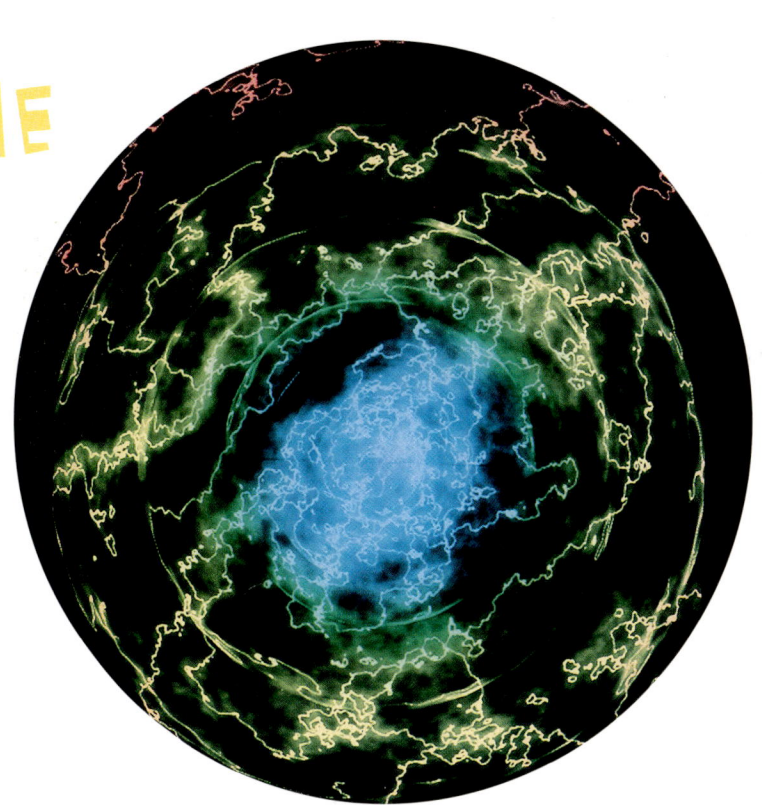

Many of the pictures in this book are called TEMs—images made with **t**ransmission **e**lectron **m**icroscopes. These pictures are produced with electrons instead of light. A transmission electron microscope sends a stream of electrons through a thin slice of something. The electrons bounce off or pass through the specimen. Depending on what they do, a pattern of light and dark is created, forming a picture. Because TEMs can magnify something 6 million times, they can show individual atoms!

TEM images are only two-dimensional, however. For a three-dimensional view, **photomicroscopists** use a SEM—scanning electron microscope. A SEM is created by moving a stream of electrons back and forth, scanning the specimen. It can show very fine details, but the maximum magnification is only 300,000 times.

Electron microscopy allows us to see tiny images, but does not allow us to capture colors. The colors you see in TEMs and SEMs are artificially created by computers. Sometimes the computer coloring is just a guess. Sometimes it shows the colors that we have seen when the microbes grow in huge colonies.

photomicroscopists (fo-to-my-CRAH-sco-pists) people who take photographs using a microscope.

SKIN

habitats (HA-beh-tats) The places or environments where a plant or animal normally lives and grows.

Beads of sweat on human skin

You are going to lose a million skin cells in the next 40 minutes. A million more will flake off in the 40 minutes after that, and again in the 40 minutes after that. Skin shedding, which continues throughout your life, is a protective device that defends you against microbes that want to invade your body. Bit by tiny bit, the entire surface of your skin is shed every 14 days, and with it go any bacteria, fungus, or virus particles that were trying to colonize you. It's an effective defense but not perfect. Many microbes survive by hiding out in the glands and pores that extend below your skin.

To a microbe, your suit of skin has **habitats** as varied as those of the earth. To them, your armpits are as warm and moist as a rain forest. Your forearms are as dry and windswept as a desert. Each of the mini environments on your 18 square feet of skin is inhabited by different microbes.

Human skin isn't a friendly place for bacteria, fungi, or viruses that have not evolved to live there. Sweat contains lactic acid and salt, which are bacteria killers. Tears have fungus-killing chemicals. And the skin microbes jealously guard their territory, using lethal **antibiotic** and antifungal weapons.

One thing that influences which species will be able to survive in the zoo on you is clothing. Your surface zoo changes with the changes in fashion. When tight clothes are common, for instance, so are microbes that like the warmer and damper environment snug-fitting clothes provide. Not wearing any clothes at all would result in a much smaller zoo. A naked body would expose the zoo on your skin to the microbe-killing ultraviolet rays in sunlight. But going naked would not be a good way to cleanse yourself of microbes, because the amount of sun necessary to kill off your covering of microorganisms would also give you a bad sunburn.

The zoo on you also depends on the availability of food. Kids have far more species of microbes in their zoo than adults do. Adults ooze fatty substances out of their skin and have mostly just a few aggressive species that want to feast on the oily goo.

> **antibiotic**
> (an-ti-bie-AH-tic)
> a chemical produced by microorganisms to kill other microorganisms. Often used by humans to fight diseases.

FACE

The human face is one tough place to live. It's exposed to weather. It's regularly washed with strong chemicals. And it's in nearly constant motion. To a microbe, it must be like living in a neighborhood that has daily floods and nonstop earthquakes. In spite of such harsh conditions, the human face has plenty of permanent residents.

Propionibacterium acnes **(PRO-pe-O-ni-back-TEER-e-um AK-nees)**

The short, plump, rod-shaped *Propionibacterium acnes* has a most unfortunate name. The mere mention of it strikes terror into the hearts of teenagers. This bacterium, once thought to be the cause of zits, has really gotten a bum rap. Even though we now know that it doesn't cause acne, it's stuck with its unpleasant name. True, you can find acne bacteria on the faces of people with pimples. But you can also find them on folks without a pimple in sight. *Propionibacterium acnes* has been found on every single person who has been checked. The average kid's face is home to more than 2 billion acne bacteria.

Acne bacteria hang out in the hair **follicles** of your face. There they munch on food that oozes out of your skin. The sludgy, butterlike goo called sebum is what they like best, and it's produced by the oil glands that lubricate your hairs. The reason for sebum is a mystery. It doesn't contain chemicals to kill microbes, prevent water loss, or guard

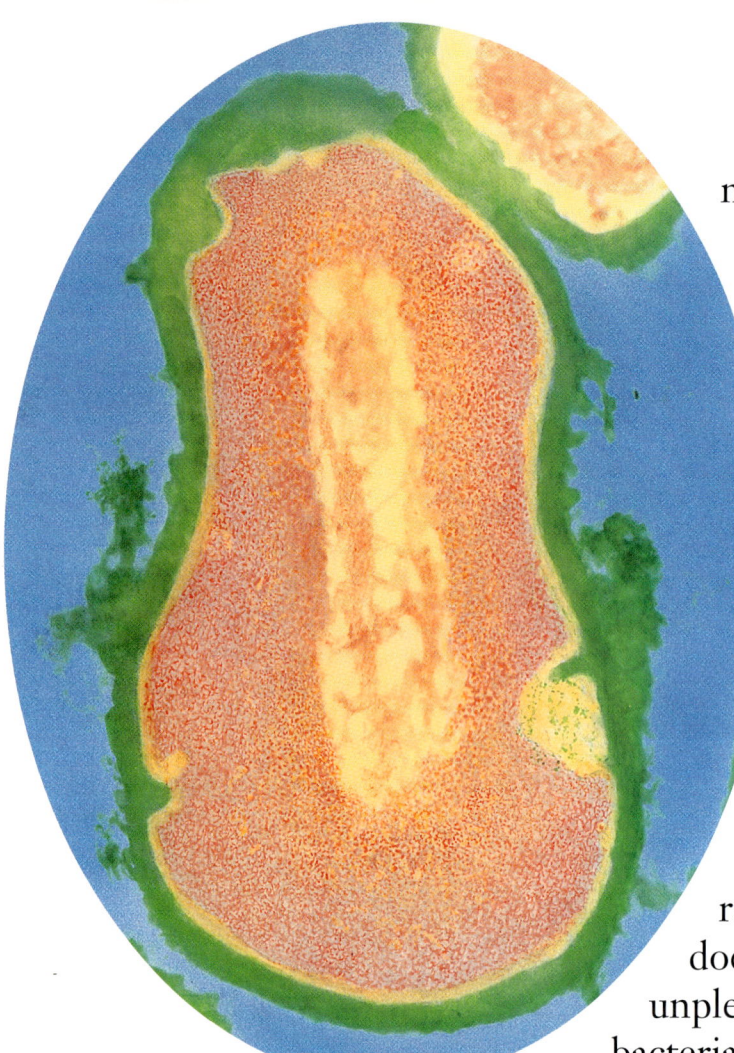

Propionibacterium acnes use acid to defend their living space against competing microbes.

follicles (FAH-li-kuls) small pits from which hair grows.

against sunburn. About the only thing it seems to do is start acne.

When you start to produce sex hormones, the sebum begins to pour out. Teenagers make so much sebum that their follicles get clogged shut. That doesn't stop the sebum production though, and it keeps pouring out until the sides of the follicle rupture under the pressure. If the normally harmless acne bacteria are trapped inside they can cause the infection that gives them their name.

Demodex folliculorum (DE-mo-dex fol-li-cu-LOR-um)

The largest inhabitants of your face are tiny parasitic animals called mites. They avoid the surface, seeking protection instead in the pits and pores of the skin. The mites' long slender shape allows them to live right inside narrow oil glands and hair follicles.

***Demodex folliculorum*, eyelash mites, are animals with external skeletons, but they are flexible enough to bend in half. Their eight pudgy, peglike legs are used to hold onto a hair while they are in its follicle. They hardly ever travel, but when necessary can toddle along, alternately moving the four legs on each side.**

Although follicle mites are thousands of times bigger than bacteria, you can't see them, and perhaps more important, you can't feel them moving around. Four of the *Demodex folliculorum* mites that live in your eyelashes could fit on the period at the end of this sentence. You're sure to host them—eventually. Eyelash mites are found on half of all elementary school kids and on all adults.

For most of their two-week life, eyelash mites live head down with a group of buddies in the dark, damp holes in your skin. There's room for up to ten mites in a single eyelash follicle. Unless it gets too crowded, there's very little reason for them to wander. Follicles and oil glands provide food as well as shelter. The mites eat sebum and the acne bacteria that live in the follicles with them.

As you read this, a billion mites are living on your face. They are breeding and laying eggs there. Don't worry. These relatives of spiders and ticks are the only animals that inhabit human skin and don't cause any damage. They are unique in that respect.

When microscopists began to study eyelash mites they discovered another unique thing about them. These tiny animals didn't appear to have an **anus**. Throughout its life, an eyelash mite eats—but nothing comes out! If you think about it, you should be very happy that your eyelash mites are missing this particular body part.

anus (A-nus) the opening at the end of the digestive system through which undigested food is eliminated.

ARMPITS

Armpits are dark and damp places—perfect for microbes. More of them live in your pits than on any other part of your skin. About 2 million microorganisms are crammed into every square centimeter of this hot spot. Some fungi and viruses are at home on the moist skin under your arms, but the zoo that lives in your pits is mostly a bacterial zoo.

Staphylococcus aureus (staf-ee-low-KAA-kus OR-ee-us)

One of the most common members of your pit crew is *Staphylococcus aureus*. Named for the shape and color of its colonies (staphylococcus= grapelike; aureus= gold), this bacterium lives on most of us as a harmless resident. Many people would describe *Staphylococcus aureus* as beneficial, because it manufactures **toxins**, substances that are poisonous to other microbes. Some of these poisons kill disease-causing bacteria; others keep flesh-eating fungi from devouring your body.

Staphylococcus live in our armpits because there's plenty of food for them there.

toxins (TOK-sins) poisonous substances produced by microorganisms, plants or animals.

These bacteria eat sweat! This is rather unfortunate, because these sweat eaters are the cause of the smell in our armpits. Fresh perspiration has almost no odor. What you smell in a stinky pit are the waste products of bacteria that have eaten your sweat. The first underarm deodorants contained antibiotics that killed the odor-causing bacteria. That was a big mistake. Without bacteria to keep them in check, fungi, which aren't killed by antibiotics, took over. The bacteria-free armpits rotted. Rotting armpits stank even worse—and they itched.

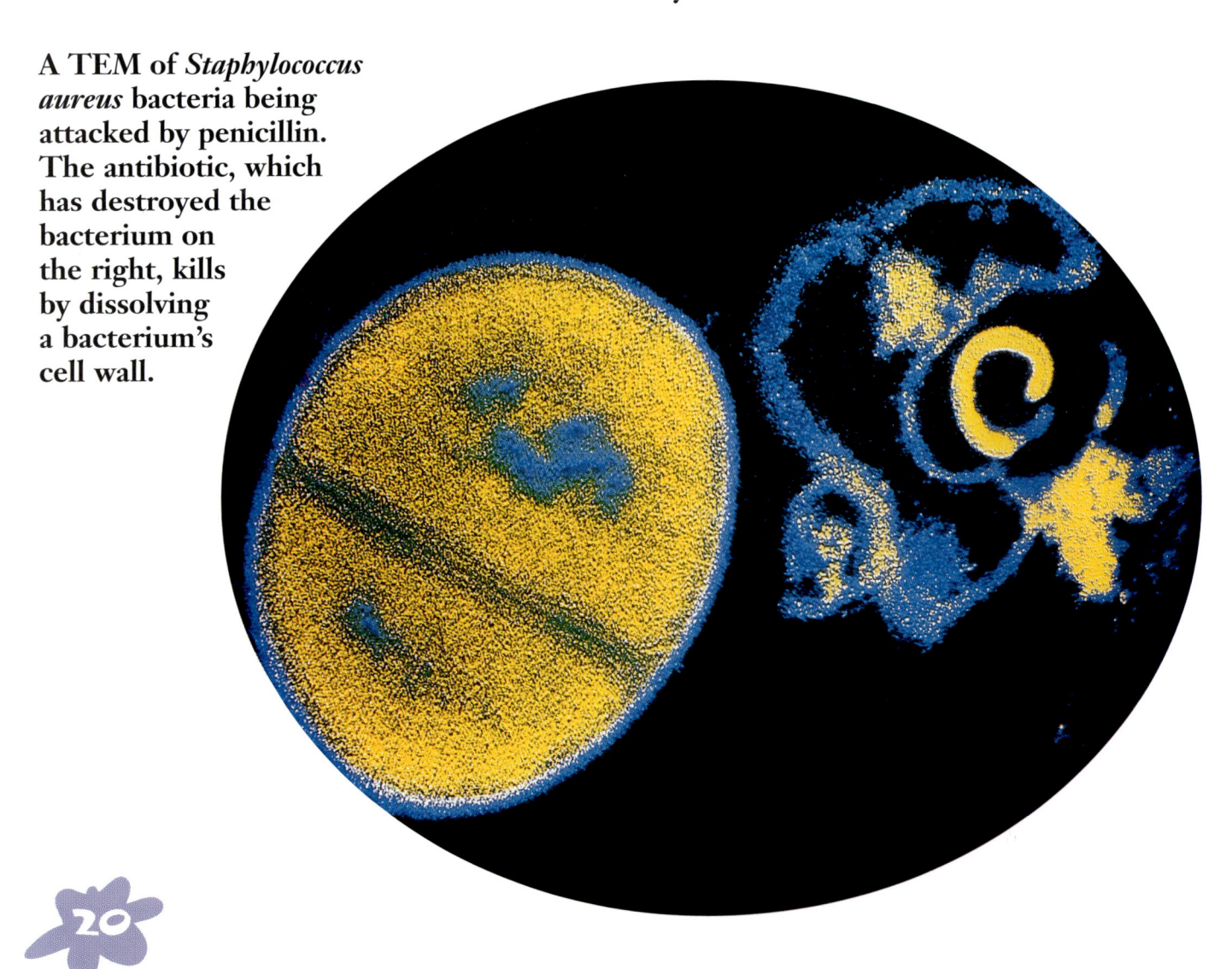

A TEM of *Staphylococcus aureus* bacteria being attacked by penicillin. The antibiotic, which has destroyed the bacterium on the right, kills by dissolving a bacterium's cell wall.

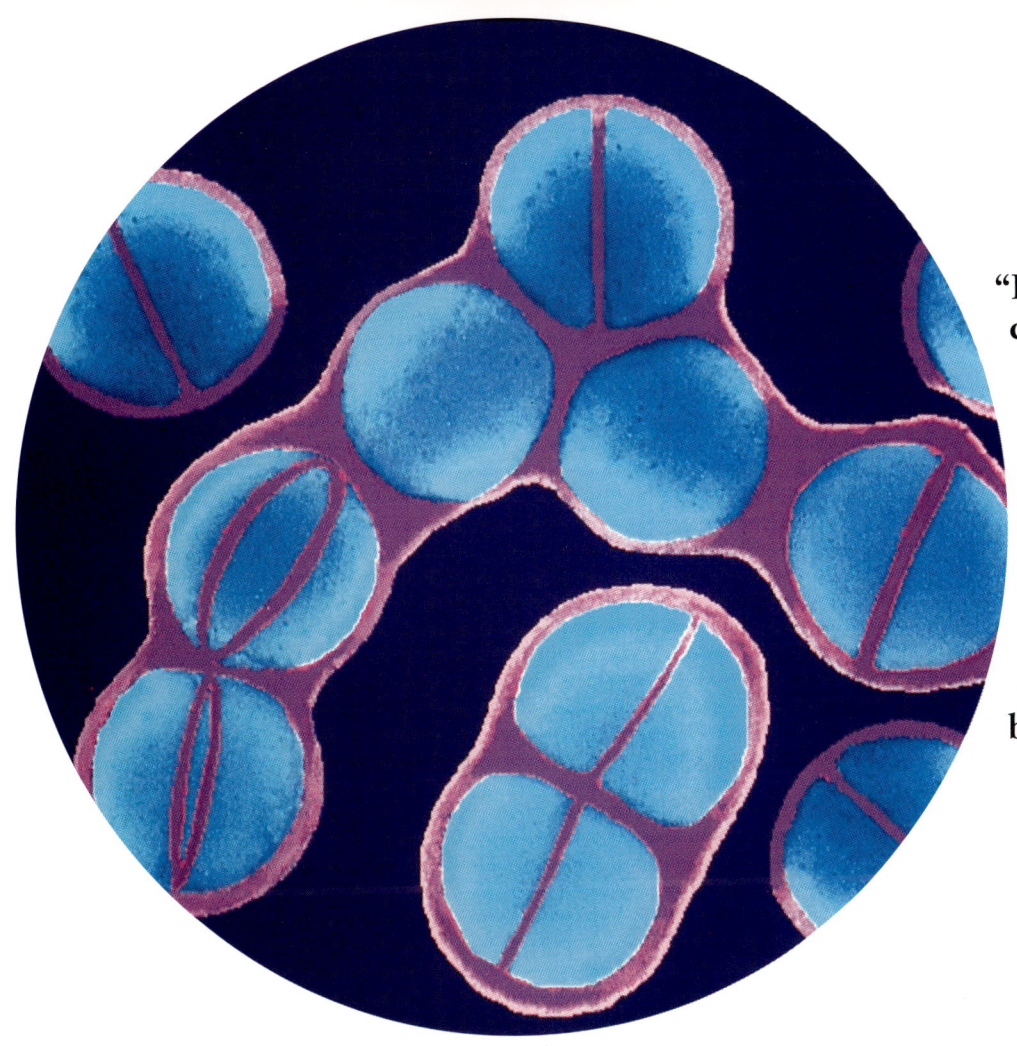

"Divide and conquer" could be the motto of *Staphylococcus aureus* bacteria. They reproduce by binary fission: First they duplicate themselves and then they pinch themselves in half, creating two smaller but complete cells.

Modern deodorants work by blocking the sweat glands with aluminum compounds. Deprived of food and moisture, neither bacteria nor fungi can survive.

Younger kids don't have many *staphylococcus aureus* bacteria, and also don't have strong body odors. Ordinary sweat, from one of your 3 million sweat glands, is basically salt water. Salt water isn't a very nutritious diet. Sweat that these bacteria use for food comes from extra-large sweat glands located in your armpits and groin. These glands, which become active only in **puberty**, contain substances that bacteria can use as food.

puberty (PU-ber-ty) The time when reproduction first becomes possible.

HANDS

Papovavirus (pa-PO-va-VI-rus)

The smallest residents in the human zoo are papovaviruses, the cause of warts. There are more than 80 different kinds of papovaviruses, and 95 percent of us are infected with one or more of them. Even so, the odds are good that you won't get a wart. Less than one percent of people with a papovavirus will get one of the tumorlike skin growths. Wart viruses are spread when we touch each other. That's why the hand is the most likely place to get a wart.

Papovaviruses have a lumpy-bumpy appearance—like the warts they produce.

Scientists don't know how most people fight off warts. And they also don't know why you are five times more likely to get warts if you are between the ages of 9 and 16, and female.

Papovaviruses, like all viruses, are **parasites**. They can wait years—thousands of years if necessary—until they find a living cell to invade. Once inside the cell, they trick their **host** into making copies of their tiny viral selves.

> **parasites** (PARE-eh-sites)
> Organisms living dependently in, with, or on other organisms without being of any benefit.

> **host** (hoest)
> The larger, stronger, dominant organism.

HAIR AND SCALP

Hair is resistant to attack by microbes. That's why mummies have been found with their hair undecayed after thousands of years. On a living body, hair is shed regularly, so microbes don't get too well established. Head hairs are renewed every 3 to 5 years. The short hairs on your body are replaced every 4 1/2 months. Eyelashes, with their 150-day life span, have the most rapid turnover.

Pityrosporum ovale (pit-ee-row-SPOR-um O-val-ee)

Dandruff is a disease of the skin, not the hair. So, yes, bald people can get dandruff. Kids can get dandruff, too, although it is not very common. There's nose dandruff and ear dandruff as well as head dandruff. Dandruff also affects many hairy animals such as cats, dogs, llamas, and horses.

The flaky disease is an allergic reaction to one of our most common skin commensals, a yeast fungi called *Pityrosporum ovale*. This fungus lives on fats such as lanolin, sebum, and earwax. It is found on the scalp and face of more than 90 percent of all humans; 70 percent of ten-year-old kids have the dandruff-causing yeasts.

Your chances of making the yeast grow fast enough for you to get dandruff are dramatically increased if you do something that puts you under stress, makes you perspire a lot, and requires the wearing of a tight-fitting hat or helmet. You won't be surprised to learn that a lot of hockey players have dandruff! Unfortunately, we don't know all the reasons why people get dandruff. The fungus just grows faster on some folks—up to three times the normal rate.

Every eighteen hours or so, *Pityrosporum* reproduces asexually by forming buds that break away from the mother cell.

FEET

Dermatophytes (der-MA-toe-fites)

It smells bad. It's itchy. It's contagious. And it attacks the skin between your toes. What is it? Fungus of the foot, better known as athlete's foot, caused by dermatophytes.

Dermatophytes means "skin plants." These moldy fungi eat our hair and skin. It's not much of an inconvenience to have molds munch on these dead bits of us, but to make sure that they don't reach our live parts we shed the skin they are living on every few weeks. If the fungi get aggressive and begin to grow faster, they irritate our skin and our skin then responds by shedding the cells faster. When the fungi are speedier than our defenses, athlete's foot happens. More than half the kids at school are walking around with one or more of the molds that cause this disease and they don't even know it.

Dermatophytes, like most fungi, grows best where it is wet. Feet are often wet because we have the habit of covering them with socks and shoes that hold in moisture. Athlete's foot does not occur among people who traditionally go barefoot.

Dermatophytes don't colonize new places by sending out spores the way other members of their moldy family do. They spread from host to host by traveling on bits of skin and hair that get caught on furniture, clothes, or gym towels.

spores (sporz)
single-celled reproductive bodies of fungi.

25

SKIN FLAKES

Dermatophagoides pteronyssinus
(DER-ma-toe-FAG-oi-dees TER-o-NIS-y-nus)

Dust mites have a hard outer shell called an exoskeleton, but they can feel things in spite of the armor. The widely spaced hairs that stick out of the exoskeleton are sensitive to touch.

Under a microscope the dust mite looks like a terrible monster, but it is a gentle, harmless creature. Although its closest relatives are spiders, scorpions, and ticks, a dust mite doesn't bite or sting. It doesn't need to. This tiny animal, a cousin of the eyelash mite, has few enemies, and its food consists of things that are already dead—dead bits of us! Dinner for a dust mite is a flake of human skin. Dander is what we call this minimeal (or dandruff, if the skin cells clump together into larger chunks). Skin flakes are tiny enough to pass easily through clothing. In fact, 90 percent of household dust is made of our own dead skin.

The chubby dander-eaters used to live right on the surface of our skin. But sometime back in the distant past, they abandoned us. It was a good move. Skin-eating mites, one of the smallest free-living animals in the world (they're about the same size as eyelash mites, a hundred to the inch) are now one of the most numerous animals.

You can find dust mites wherever people live, but the largest concentration is in the bedroom. It may gross you out to know that you probably share your mattress with 50 million mites. And 20 percent of the weight of your pillow is most likely made up of dust mites and their droppings. For those who are not allergic, living with mites is no problem. But many people get an allergic reaction to mites' pollen-size droppings. There is no shortage of droppings. In a mite's six-week lifetime it produces 200 times its own body weight in **feces**.

The dust mite's eight stumpy legs have tiny hooks that help it hold onto bedding and carpets.

feces (FEE-sees) solid waste from the digestive canal.

AIRWAYS

The nose, bronchial tubes, and lungs have protective devices to kill the armies of microbes that are carried into our breathing passages with every gulp of air. The nose is lined with hairs that trap small airborne particles that might be carrying bacteria. If the hairs are overwhelmed by an enormous number of particles, a sneeze will send the intruders flying. Coughing, a similar action, expels microbes that have invaded deeper passages.

Most of the normal flora of the airways are found in the nose. The airway policing system is so effective that the bronchial tubes and the lungs are usually free of microbes.

Streptococcus viridans (STREP-tuh-KAA-kus veer-rid-ans)

King of the airways, *Streptococcus viridans* is the most common bacteria in the nose, throat, and mouth. Normally harmless, it produces no toxins and is easily destroyed by white blood cells if it should find a way into our body tissues. There is one rather serious exception to this. If the bacteria get into the bloodstream and reach a heart that is already damaged, they can cause a fatal infection. Here's what happens. One or more of the bacteria catch on a rough spot of the injured heart and become covered by a blood clot before the white blood cells can find and destroy them. When the blood clot breaks loose it carries the viridans bacteria throughout the body.

Tonsils are the headquarters for *Streptococcus viridans* bacteria, a member of the normal flora of the breathing passages. This SEM shows the typical paired formation of the species.

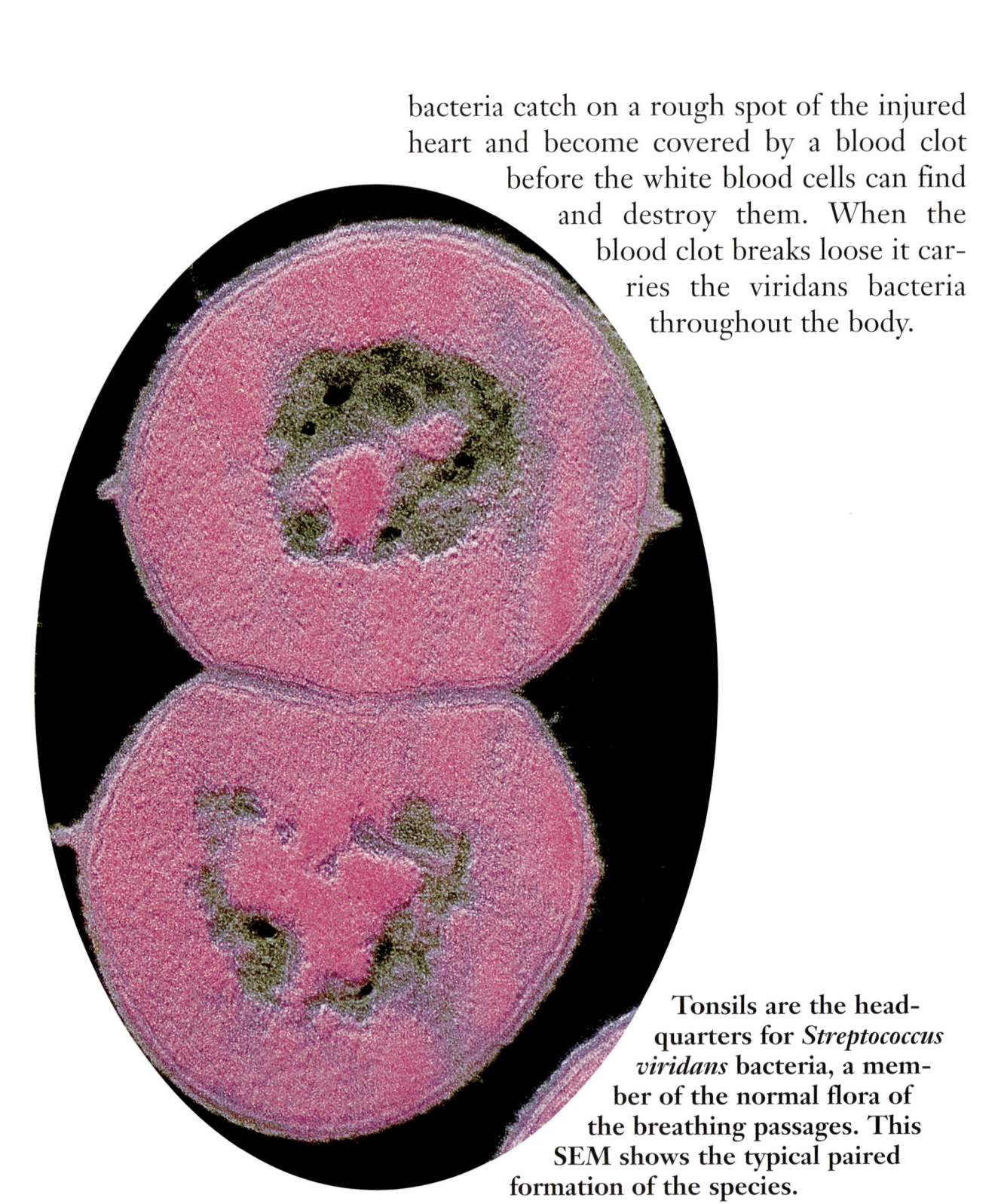

MOUTH

Spit kills! Saliva has antibodies in it that kill organisms that cause tooth decay. You can produce as much as two quarts of saliva every day. Your mouth is a very busy place. It is home to 400 to 500 different species of microorganisms. The normal flora includes helpful microbes. Some aid in digesting food. Others keep more dangerous germs away. Unfortunately, many of our microbes make acid wastes that can lead to tooth decay, which is why we need to brush them away.

Saliva is not a simple watery fluid. It is a delivery system for a whole range of chemical weapons. The inside of the mouth constantly monitors what's going on, and the saliva glands add or subtract chemicals as needed. They can add substances to spit that bind with acids that bacteria make; they can produce **sodium bicarbonate** to neutralize mouth acid or even trick teeth-hugging bacteria into producing **alkaline** substances instead of acids.

If you can't kill a microorganism with spit, you could slime it to death. All the parts of the body that are exposed to the environment (except the skin) have a protective lining of mucus, that slimy sticky stuff no one likes to talk about. The inside of the mouth is coated with

---

sodium bicarbonate (SO-dee-um bi-CAR-bo-nate) baking soda.

alkaline (AL-ka-line) neutral, as opposed to acidic.

mucus, which prevents the microbes from getting a "grip" and making a home for themselves. Saliva can clump them together into harmless lumps, which are then swallowed.

TONGUE

The rough surface of the tongue is an ideal breeding ground for bacteria. Most of the ones that call your tongue home have special surfaces that enable them to hold on.

A color enhanced SEM of a human tongue

***Actinomyces israelii* (ak-tin-o-MY-sees is-RAIL-ee)**

Commonly called the "bad breath bug," *Actinomyces israelii*, is actually quite helpful. A member of your normal tongue flora, this rod-shaped bacteria aids in digestion by breaking proteins into usable substances. The help has a price—bad breath. One of the by-products of their breakdown of proteins is sulfur in the form of hydrogen sulfide gas, a really foul-smelling compound.

Actinomycetes bacteria are found in their greatest numbers on the tongue. So if you want to get rid of bad breath, brush your tongue.

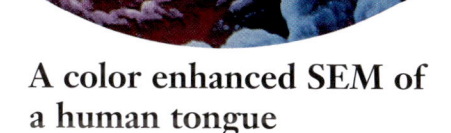

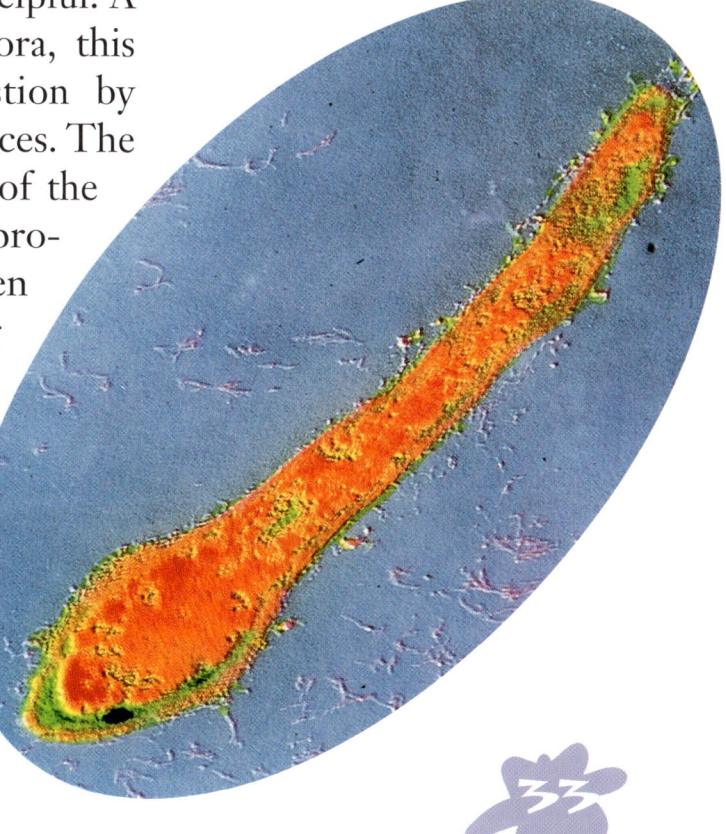

TEETH

Certain types of bacteria can attach themselves to hard surfaces like the enamel that covers your teeth. These bacteria turn sugar into a kind of glue that they use to stick themselves to a tooth and to each other. If they're not removed, they multiply into a colony. Proteins in your saliva also mix in, and the bacterial colony becomes a whitish film called **plaque**. The waste products of the plaque bacteria are acids that dissolve your tooth enamel. Saliva works hard by bringing new minerals to repair the damage. But if the plaque is thick, it prevents saliva from reaching the damaged surfaces and eventually the bacterial acids eat through the enamel and expose the tender living parts of the tooth. When this happens your body can no longer repair the damage—only a dentist can.

Entamoeba gingivalis (en-tuh-MEE-buh JIN-ji-val-is)

There's a real-life shape shifter in your mouth—an **amoeba**. It probably got there in the saliva of a kiss. Teenagers most often get amoebas from a human-to-human smooch; younger kids from doggy kisses.

The red rods are bacteria on the surface of a human tooth.

plaque (plak) a mixture of bacteria and saliva proteins that forms on teeth.

amoeba (uh-MEE-buh) a one-celled animal in the protozoa family.

Plaque is a white film that forms on your teeth. It is a yucky mix of bacteria, old food, saliva, and macrophages, which have been sent to destroy the bacteria by eating them.

Tooth amoebas are active hunters that capture their prey with the same **pseudopods** that they use to move. Bacteria are the meat they seek. They do you a favor by eating as many tooth-destroying microbes as they can.

Members of the protozoa family, amoebas constantly change their shape as they move. The helpful *Entamoeba gingivalis* is found in about half of human mouths. Although it is a thousand times larger than a bacterium, it's hard to get rid of a tooth amoeba with a brush. There are a lot of small places in the mouth for a microscopic shape-shifting amoeba to hide.

pseudopod
(SU-do-pod) false foot.

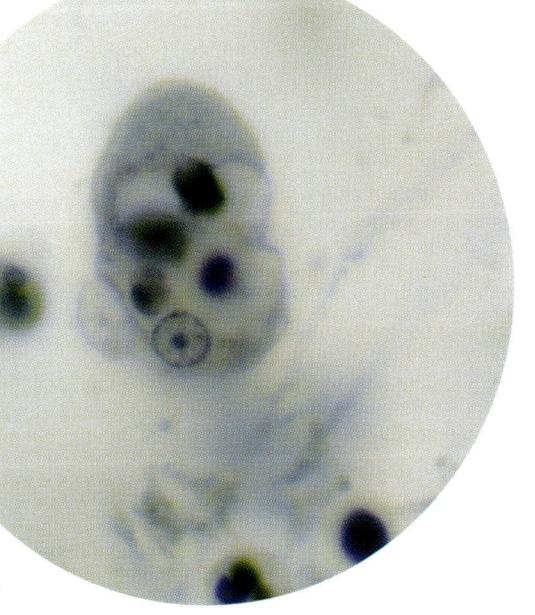

Amoeba have been around for almost two billion years. *Entamoeba gingivalis* is a harmless member of our normal mouth flora. It's one of six different species of amoeba that are parasites of the human mouth and intestines.

Most of the zoo on you lives in the 30-foot canal that goes from your mouth to your anus. Strictly speaking, the microorganisms of your stomach and intestines aren't "inside" your body. Both ends of your food tube are open, so technically, your guts are just a hole through the center of your body.

Wet, dark, and without much oxygen, the gut is a different environment from the rest of your body's surface. It's definitely a microbe-friendly neighborhood. More than 500 kinds of bacteria and several dozen assorted protozoa, yeasts, molds, and viruses are members of the normal flora of the gut. If you scraped all your gutsy bugs together they would fill a soup can. In contrast, all the rest of your zoo would fit in a thimble.

A **zillion** of your bacteria buddies pass out of your body in every

zillion (ZIL-yun) not an exact number. It means a large number. If you want a more accurate count of the number of bacteria leaving your body, figure ten trillion (10,000,000,000,000) for each thimbleful of waste.

Microorganisms don't have muscles, but they are able to swim through the liquid contents of the guts with whiplike appendages called flagella that are powered by a chemical called ATP, short for adenosine triphosphate. Bacteria, protozoa, and even human sperm cells use this method to move around.

bowel movement. About half of your feces consists of the bodies of bacteria!

STOMACH

The stomach produces such strong acid to digest food that it is also an effective germ barrier. It's not easy to live in hydrochloric acid. Very few microorganisms—helpful or dangerous—are able to survive even a quick trip through the stomach.

Lactobacillus acidophilus
(lac-toe-ba-CILL-us a-sid-AH-fuh-lus)

Unlike most microbes, the lactobacillus bacteria found in yogurt can live in an acid environment. Every time you eat a container of yogurt, you swallow billions of these helpful bacteria, and they pass into the intestines unharmed. Once in the intestines, these rod-shaped bacteria cling to the walls and begin to eat bits of sugary foods that pass by. Lactic acid is one of their waste products. Far from hurting you, the acid wastes of the lactobacilli protect you by driving off harmful microbes.

You need these helpful bacteria in your intestines. If you take an antibiotic to eliminate other bacteria that are making you sick, you also kill off the good lactobacteria. Without your "protector" bacteria, you are in for a fight. Antibiotics don't kill fungi, and without

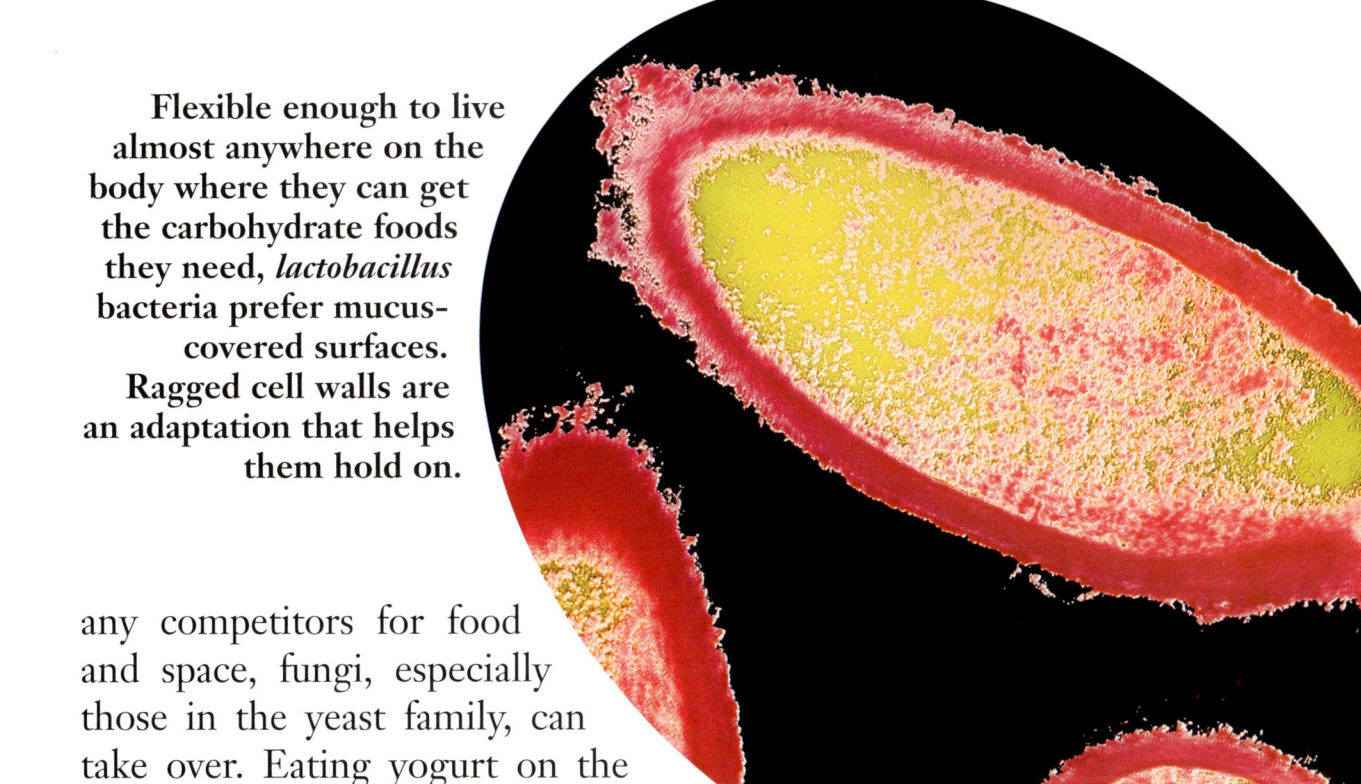

Flexible enough to live almost anywhere on the body where they can get the carbohydrate foods they need, *lactobacillus* bacteria prefer mucus-covered surfaces. Ragged cell walls are an adaptation that helps them hold on.

any competitors for food and space, fungi, especially those in the yeast family, can take over. Eating yogurt on the days you're taking antibiotics is a good idea.

INTESTINES

Bacteria are everywhere there is food—and humans are food. But so are bacteria! In our intestines, bacteria sometimes become one snack. By digesting some of our microbial companions we add protein to our diet. But making a meal of our resident microbes is a bit like eating the goose that laid the golden egg. Without them the lining of our intestines wouldn't develop correctly, and it would be impossible to digest other food properly. Luckily, there are enough to go around for every need.

Escherichia coli **(esh-uh-R-EESH-uh KO-lie)**

The dominant organism in the human gut is a rod-shaped bacterium with a tongue-twisting name, *Escherichia coli*. There are many different strains or families of *E. coli*, as scientists call it for short. The majority are harmless to most humans most of the time. But when we travel, even to the next state, we meet new families of these bacteria sometimes, and they usually cause diarrhea until our immune system adapts to them.

E. coli are capable of reproducing at astronomical rates. A single bacterium could multiply into a mass greater than the earth in three days if enough food were available.

There's plenty of food available to *E. coli* in your intestines. A lot of it is stuff you couldn't digest. Waste to you, these leftover fibers are

Bacteria reproduce by dividing or budding. However, in 1946, it was discovered that some kinds of bacteria could also mate with each other. This TEM shows three *E. coli* bacteria, a male and two females, exchanging DNA. Both sexes give and receive genetic material through the male's long hollow hairs called F-pili.

E. coli are one of the fastest-multiplying organisms, doubling in number every 20 minutes if conditions are favorable. Not all microorganisms separate at division. As you can see here, they may stay attached or form chains or clumps.

yummy food to *E. coli*. In turn, some of the waste products of *E. coli* are chemicals you need but can't make for yourself. The intestines quickly soak up *E. coli*–created vitamin K, for without it blood would not clot when you cut yourself. Vitamin B_{12} (which is really folic acid and not a vitamin) is sent to the liver, where it is stored to protect against memory loss, blood diseases, birth defects, and a lot of other serious problems. Your liver can store a 5-year supply of B_{12}. So, you not only have to feed your body to stay healthy, you have to feed your body's bacteria, too!

Before we leave the intestines, there is something else about these bacterial buddies that must be mentioned. Gas! *E. coli* is the leading cause of farts. Foods such as beans, cabbage, and brussels sprouts cannot be digested by humans but can be digested by *E.*

coli and other microbes. One of their wastes is methane gas, the cause of the greenhouse effect in the atmosphere. Another waste product, hydrogen sulfide gas, is what gives intestinal gas its distinctive odor. You pump out a quart of gas every day—even more if you are fond of beans.

Streptococcus faecalis (STREP-tuh-KAA-kus FEE-kal-iss)

The sphere-shaped *Streptococcus faecalis* are bacteria with a Jekyll-and-Hyde nature. Common and harmless in the intestines, these microbes turn into deadly threats if they gain entry into our body tissues. These bacteria are why a burst appendix is so dangerous. Many members of the streptococcus family produce an enzyme that dissolves the tissues that bind skin to muscle. An infection of these "flesh-eating bacteria" can devour your body at the rate of one inch an hour.

A colony of streptococcus bacteria showing the "chain of berries" formation that gave the family its name. *Streptococcus faecalis* is one of the most common commensals of the large intestines of humans and other mammals.

Candida albicans
(CAN-dee-duh AL-bee-kans)

Not all gut microbes are bacteria. There is a fungus among us. This one-celled member of the yeast branch of the fungus family is usually kept from multiplying too rapidly by our immune system and candida's archenemy, the bacterium *Lactobacillus acidophilus*, the one that makes yogurt.

A colony of the yeast, *Candida albicans*, a resident of most of your mucus membranes. With its smell of rotting fish, this yeast could just as easily have been named stinkus.

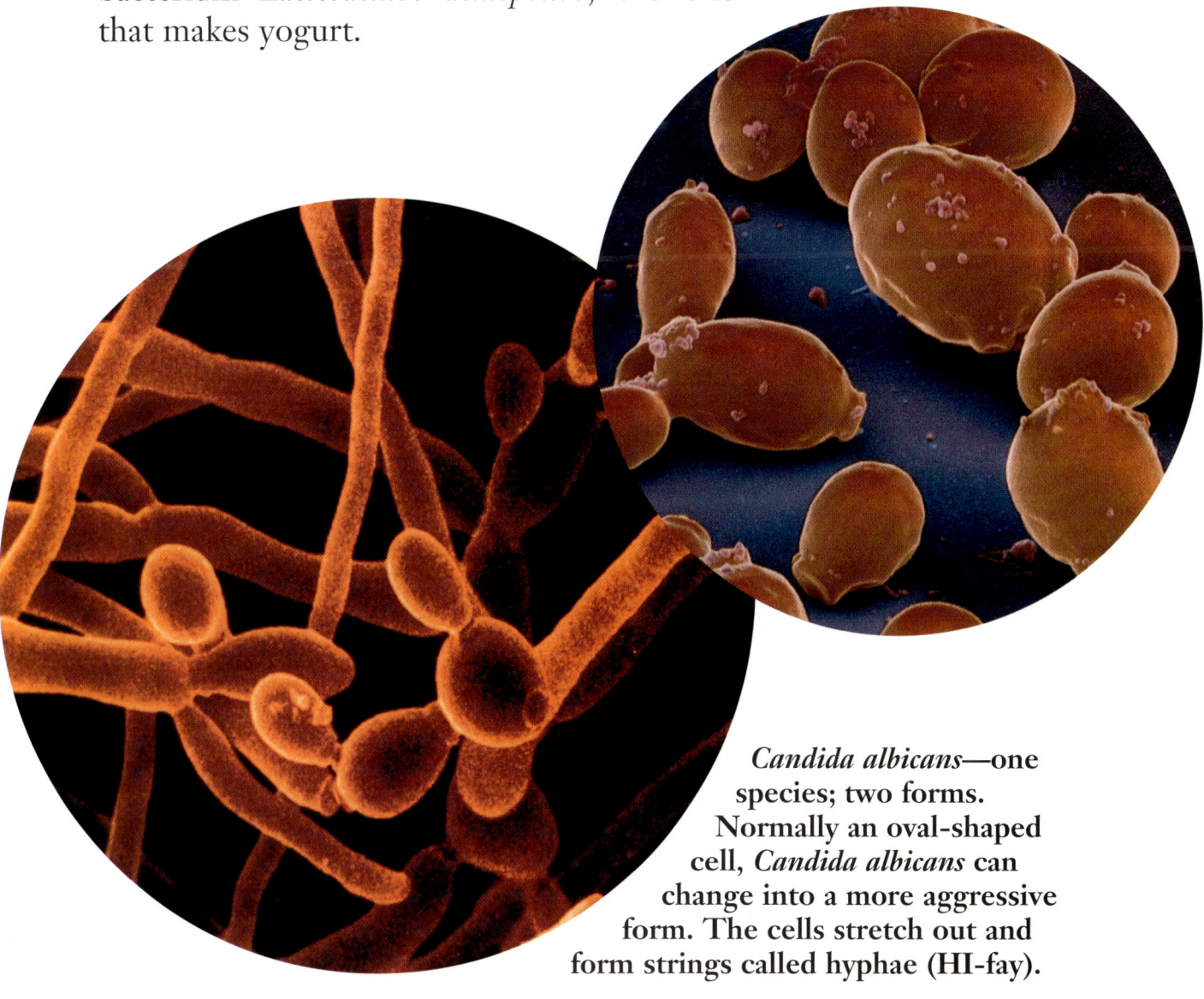

Candida albicans—one species; two forms. Normally an oval-shaped cell, *Candida albicans* can change into a more aggressive form. The cells stretch out and form strings called hyphae (HI-fay).

DANGEROUS WEAPONS

The war between microbes has been going on for millions—perhaps billions—of years. During that time the little creatures have created some really impressive chemical weapons. Humans know a good thing when they see it and have borrowed the most powerful of these poisons to use against their own disease-causing enemies.

Penicillin, the first antibiotic, was produced from a mold. The bacteria-fighting medicines, bacitracin and polymyxin, are made by bacteria. Cyclosporin, another antibiotic, is a mold-made substance that kills bacteria with a chemical that dissolves their cell walls.

Antibiotics are not a final solution in the fight against microbes. Living organisms, even bacteria and fungi, adapt to survive. When you take an antibiotic medicine, some of the bacteria infecting you will survive. We call these survivors drug-resistant bacteria.

There are two ways bacteria can become resistant to antibiotics. One is spontaneous mutation, caused by a mistake in the copying of DNA information. The other type of drug resistance was discovered in 1959 by Japanese bacteriologists who were studying spontaneous mutations. They found, unfortunately for us, that the ability to resist an antibiotic doesn't stay locked inside a mutated bacteria. It is concentrated in tough coils that are pushed out through the bacteria's surface and absorbed inside nearby bacteria even if they are of a different species!

This transferable resistance is particularly common among bacteria that live in the guts of humans and animals. In addition to the antibiotics we take when we're sick, we get antibiotics in our food. (Farmers give antibiotics to healthy livestock, not to prevent diseases, but because antibiotics boost the animals' growth.) So, we are dosed with antibiotics almost every day. Some of our normal flora become drug resistant. That's not a problem. However, if they transfer the resistance to dangerous disease-causing organisms, that is a serious problem, for there are now germs that are resistant to all known drugs.

Don't count humans out, though. We are experts at survival. The zoo on you is watched over by a remarkable zookeeper—your immune system. Always adapting, it can produce new kinds of antibodies to protect you when dangerous microbes attack. And humans have an advantage over all other living things with a second line of defense—science. With technology we have the power to create biological defense weapons using techniques such as gene splicing and recombining DNA.

INDEX

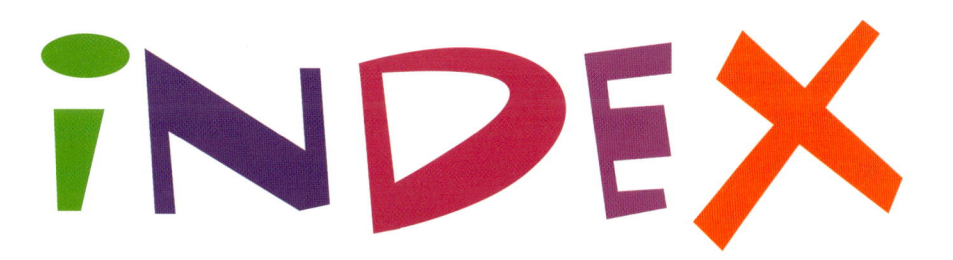

Acne, 16–18
Actinomyces israelii, 33
Alkaline substances, 32
Allergies, 27
Amoebas, 10, 34–35
Animals, 8, 9
Antibiotics, 15, 20, 38, 45–46
Antibodies, 5
Anus, 18
Armpits, 19–21
Athlete's foot, 25
ATP (adenosine triphosphate), 37

Bacitracin, 45
Bacteria, defined, 4
Bad breath, 33
Body oils, 5
Bronchial tubes, 29

Candida albicans, 43
Cleanliness, 6
Clothing, 15
Colonies of microbes, 4
Commensals, defined, 6
Coughing, 29
Cyclosporin, 45

Dander, 26
Dandruff, 23–24, 26
Deficiencies, vitamin, 4–5
Demodex folliculorum, 17–18

Deodorants, 20–21
Dermatophytes, 25
Diarrhea, 40
DNA, 45, 46
Drug-resistant bacteria, 45–46
Dust mites, 26–27

Ear wax, 24
Electron microscopy, 11–12
Entamoeba gingivalis, 34, 35
Escherichia coli, 8, 40–42
Exoskeleton, 26
Eyelash mites, 17–18, 26

Face, 15–18
Feces, 27, 38
Feet, 25
Flagella, 37
Flora, 5
Folic acid, 41
Follicles, 16–18
F-pili, 40
Fungi, 8, 9, 14, 20, 24, 25, 38–39, 43, 45

Gas, 41–42
Gene splicing, 46
Germs, 6
Greenhouse effect, 42
Gut
   intestines, 37, 39–43

   stomach, 38–39
Habitats, 14
Hair and scalp, 23–24
Hands, 22–23
Host, 23
Hydrochloric acid, 38
Hydrogen sulfide gas, 33, 42
Hyphae, 43

Immune system, 5, 40, 46
Intestines, 37, 39–43

Lactic acid, 14, 38
Lactobacillus acidophilus, 38, 39, 43
Lactobacillus bulgaricus, 6
Lanolin, 24
Liver, 41
Lungs, 29

Macrophages, 35
Metazoa, 9
Methane gas, 42
Microbes, defined, 4
Microbial cells, 4
Microns, 10
Microorganisms, defined, 4
Mites, 10, 11
   dust, 26–27
   eyelash, 17–18, 26
Molds, 4, 9, 25, 37, 45
Monera, 8
Mouth, 5

saliva, 32
teeth, 34–35
tongue, 33
Mucus, 32–33
Mummies, 23
Mushrooms, 9

Nose, 5, 29

Oil glands, 16, 18
Organisms, defined, 9

Papovavirus, 22–23
Parasites, 23
Pathogens, 5
Penicillin, 20, 43
Photomicroscopists, 12
Pityrosporum ovale, 23–24
Plants, 8, 9
Plaque, 34, 35
Polymyxin, 45
Propionibacterium acnes, 16–18
Protista, 8, 9
Protozoa, 9, 35, 37
Pseudopods, 35
Puberty, 21

Recombining DNA, 46

Saliva, 32–34
Sebum, 16–17, 24
SEMs (scanning electron microscopes), 12
Sex hormones, 17
Skin, 14–23
 armpits, 19–21
 face, 15–18
 feet, 25
 flakes, 26–27
 hair and scalp, 23–24
 hands, 22–23
Sneezing, 29
Sodium bicarbonate, 32
Sperm cells, 37
Spontaneous mutation, 45
Spores, 25
Square centimeter, 11
Staphylococcus aureus, 19–21
Stomach, 38–39
Streptococcus faecalis, 42
Streptococcus pyogenes, 5
Streptococcus viridans, 29–30
Sunlight, 15
Sweat, 5, 14, 20–21

Tears, 14
Teeth, 34–35
TEMs (transmission electron microscopes), 11–12
Toadstools, 9
Tongue, 33
Tonsils, 30
Tooth decay, 32
Toxins, 19

Ultraviolet rays, 15

Viruses, 8–11, 14, 37
Vitamin B_{12}, 41
Vitamin deficiencies, 4–5
Vitamin K, 41

Warts, 10, 22–23
Washing, 5
White blood cells, 29, 30, 35

Yeasts, 4, 9, 10, 24, 37, 39, 43
Yogurt, 38

Zillion, defined, 37

Zits, 16